Contents

Written by
Alison Hawes

Illustrated by
Ollie Cuthbertson

Series editor **Dee Reid**

Heinemann
Part of Pearson

Characters

Salan

The King

The Green
Dragon

Tricky words

- maze
- tunnels
- sling
- rabbits
- roars
- charges

Read these words to the student. Help them with these words when they appear in the text.

Introduction

Salan is a slave. He wants to be free. But the evil King will only grant Salan his freedom if he can do four difficult and dangerous tasks.

One of Salan's tasks is to find the Green Dragon and take one of its fangs back to the King.

THE DRAGON'S FANG

Salan must find the Green Dragon and take one of its fangs to the King. The dragon lives deep inside a maze of tunnels.

Salan finds the maze of tunnels.
He takes his sling and kills two rabbits.
He cooks one rabbit over a fire and eats it.
Then he puts the other rabbit in his bag.

The dragon is too big for Salan to kill.
He must have a plan to get one of the
dragon's fangs.

Salan looks at the rabbit in his bag.
Now he has a plan.
He goes to the maze of tunnels.

Salan looks for some stones.
The stones will be in his plan.
Now he is ready for the dragon.

Salan goes deep inside the tunnels to find the dragon.

The dragon can hear Salan
but it cannot see him.
It roars down the tunnel!

Then the dragon charges down the tunnel but Salan is ready for him.
He throws the rabbit at the dragon.

The dragon eats the rabbit.
Then the dragon roars in pain.
Salan has put the stones inside the rabbit.
The dragon's fangs snap on the stones!

Salan grabs a fang and charges
out of the tunnels.
He will take the fang to the King.
Then soon, he will be free.

Quiz

Text comprehension

Literal comprehension
p5 Why doesn't Salan just kill the dragon with his sword?
p10–11 How does Salan get one of the dragon's fangs?

Inferential comprehension
p7 Why doesn't the author tell us Salan's plan?
p9 Why can't the dragon see Salan?
p12 Why does Salan charge out of the tunnel?

Personal response
• Did you guess what Salan was going to do with the rabbit and the stones?
• Do you think Salan's trick with the rabbit is clever? Why?

Word knowledge

p4 How many sentences are there on this page?
p9 Find three verbs.
p10 Which verb describes how the dragon moves down the tunnel?

Spelling challenge

Read these words:

down   give   new

Now try to spell them!

Ha! Ha! Ha!

Why did the dinosaur live longer than the dragon?

Because it didn't smoke!

Before reading Fangs

Find out about

- how some animals use their long, sharp fangs to kill their prey.

Tricky words

- prey
- hollow
- poison
- another
- sabre-tooth tigers
- centimetres
- people

Read these words to the student. Help them with these words when they appear in the text.

Introduction

Fangs are long, sharp teeth. Animals use their fangs to kill their prey. Snakes have hollow fangs. They use their hollow fangs to inject poison into their prey. Sabre-tooth tigers lived long ago. Their fangs were up to 28cm long.

14

FANGS

Fangs are long, sharp teeth. Some animals, like this wolf, use their fangs to grab and kill their prey.

Snakes

Some snakes have fangs, too. But their fangs are long, sharp and hollow.
The snakes use their hollow fangs to inject poison into their prey. If a fang snaps off, the snake can grow another fang!

Some snakes can even
spit poison from their fangs.
They can spit the poison up to
2 metres.

Sabre-tooth tigers

Sabre-tooth tigers lived long ago.
Their fangs were up to 28 centimetres long!

KILL

Sabre-tooth tigers used their fangs to grab, kill and eat big animals, like deer and horses.

Spiders

Some spiders have fangs.
They use their fangs to inject poison into
their prey.
The poison from a Red Back Spider's fangs
can even kill **people!**

Wolf spiders have no web.
So, they have to run and grab their prey, like a wolf.
Then they use their fangs to poison their prey.

Vampires

Some people are big fans of vampire films,
like the Dracula and Twilight films.
Vampires use their hollow fangs to suck blood
from their victims.

FANGS

Some fans of the Twilight films like to wear vampire teeth on top of their own teeth.

Quiz

Text comprehension

Literal

p16 What happens if a snake's fang breaks off?

p21 How do wolf spiders get their prey?

Inferential comprehension

p16 Why is it useful for a snake to grow another fang?

p17 Why is it useful for some snakes to be able to spit poison?

p20 Do all spiders have fangs?

Personal response

• Are you scared of snakes or spiders?

• Do you like vampire films? Why do you think they are popular?

Word knowledge

p15 Which two adjectives describe fangs?

p15 Find a word that rhymes with 'they'.

p16 Find three examples of different punctuation.

Spelling challenge

Read these words:

some   like   made

Now try to spell them!

Ha! Ha! Ha!

What do you get when you cross a snowman with a vampire?

Frostbite!